AUDITORY SEQUENTIAL MEMORY

INSTRUCTIONAL

WORKBOOK

**For the Development of
Auditory Listening, Processing and Recall of
Numbers, Letters and Words**

By Addie Cusimano, MEd

Auditory Sequential Memory
Instructional Workbook
For the Development of Auditory Listening, Processing and Recall of
Numbers, Letters and Words
By Addie Cusimano

Copyright© 2005 by Addie Cusimano All Rights Reserved

ISBN-10: 0-97277-623-0
ISBN-13: 978-0-97277-623-3

With the exception of the *Auditory Sequential Memory Record Sheet* that is granted special permission for copying, no part of this publication may be reproduced, stored in a retrieval system, or transmitted in any form or by any means, electronic, mechanical, photocopying, recording or otherwise, without the prior written permission of the author.

Achieve Publications
Lansdale, PA 19446
USA
www.achievepublications.com

AUDITORY SEQUENTIAL MEMORY INSTRUCTIONAL WORKBOOK

TABLE OF CONTENTS

	PAGE
EXPLANATION	i
DIRECTIONS	iii
NUMBERS	
SINGLE DIGIT NUMBERS:	
One Digit Number	1
Two, Single Digit Numbers	3
Three, Single Digit Numbers	5
Four, Single Digit Numbers	7
Five, Single Digit Numbers	9
Six, Single Digit Numbers	11
Seven, Single Digit Numbers	13
DOUBLE DIGIT NUMBERS:	
One, Two Digit Number	15
Two, Two Digit Numbers	17
Three, Two Digit Numbers	19
TRIPLE DIGIT NUMBERS:	
One, Three Digit Number	21
Two, Three Digit Numbers	23
Three, Three Digit Numbers	26
LETTERS	
One Letter	29
Two Letter Series	31
Three Letter Series	33
Four Letter Series	35
Five Letter Series	37
Six Letter Series	39
Seven Letter Series	41
WORDS	
ONE SYLLABLE WORDS:	
One, One Syllable Word	43
Two, One Syllable Words	45
Three, One Syllable Words	47
Four, One Syllable Words	49
Five, One Syllable Words	51
Six, One Syllable Words	53

AUDITORY SEQUENTIAL MEMORY INSTRUCTIONAL WORKBOOK

TABLE OF CONTENTS

TWO SYLLABLE WORDS:	
One, Two Syllable Word	55
Two, Two Syllable Words	57
Three, Two Syllable Words	59
Four, Two Syllable Words	61
Five, Two Syllable or Compound Words	63
Six, Two Syllable or Compound Words	65
AUDITORY SEQUENTIAL MEMORY RECORD SHEET Last	Page

AUDITORY SEQUENTIAL MEMORY INSTRUCTIONAL WORKBOOK

EXPLANATION:

It has been determined that each aspect of memory is specific to itself. One part of the brain controls listening for isolated units of information such as a series of numbers, letters and words. Another part of the brain controls listening for information presented in context such as information presented in a sentence that makes sense. While much of what a student hears in school is presented in context, a sizable portion is not presented in context. Therefore, a student must develop the ability to attend, listen and recall information presented in a series. This can then be applied to the learning of such skills as memorization of mathematical number facts, the spelling of words and the recall of lists of words for social studies and science.

It has also been determined that within the area of the brain that processes information in isolation or sequential order, each aspect (numbers, letters, and words) is specific to itself. Therefore, a student who has mastered the skill of number memory may not have developed the skill of remembering letters and words, or visa versa. For this reason, it is essential to consider the development of all three areas (numbers, letters and words) separately. Remediation must be done by starting at the level that is comfortable for the student, and then gradually increasing, in a developmental fashion, the amount of information to which the student can attend and recall.

While the use of diagnostic tests is the best way to determine if a student has an auditory sequential memory weakness, there are other signs that can indicate a weakness in this area. For example, when a student is working on a writing assignment and asks to have a word spelled, if the teacher has to spell the word slowly, letter by letter or two letters at a time, because the student is unable to attend and hold a longer series of letters in his mind, this is a clear indication that the student needs to expand his auditory sequential memory of letters.

When we hold a series of numbers, letters or words in our minds, it is easier to grasp and retain this information if we group the series into smaller segments of two, three or four units. For example, when we learn a telephone number, we typically group a ten digit number into segments of three, three, and four units. As a result, the numbers, 5559321426, form a grouping of 555-932-1426, an easily achievable series of numbers to recall. Likewise, when we spell words orally to someone, we often pause between the segments. For example, when someone asks us how to spell the word, *apple,* we typically group it into two separate units of two and three letters, and spell it as *ap ple*. A word like *disembark* might be grouped into

i

AUDITORY SEQUENTIAL MEMORY INSTRUCTIONAL WORKBOOK

three separate units of three, two and four letters, and spelled as *dis em bark*. As a student expands his auditory letter memory and learns how to group letters in terms of common word parts and syllables, he will be able to retain a longer and longer series of letters thus making it easier for him to recall and write more lengthy words. In addition, if a student is taught to expand his auditory sequential memory of words, he will find it easier to grasp more lengthy series of words when they are presented during classroom lectures. For example, a series of three words in science might be presented as plants needing *sun, water* and *soil* to grow, or in social studies as the five great lakes, *Huron, Ontario, Michigan, Erie,* and *Superior*. The five great lakes might be recalled in a three, two series of *Huron, Ontario, Michigan* and then *Erie, Superior*.

This *Auditory Sequential Memory Instructional Workbook* has been carefully designed to aid the teacher or parent in helping students to develop their auditory memory for a series of numbers, letters, and words in a developmental fashion. *It can be used developmentally with students from preschool to grade four. It is remedially appropriate for students in grades one through twelve and adults.*

Note:
This teaching material is also highly effective for students who exhibit *tolerance fading memory* which involves a deficiency in being able to hold in one's mind the preceding orally presented item or items of a series when the next item in the series is orally presented.

AUDITORY SEQUENTIAL MEMORY INSTRUCTIONAL WORKBOOK

DIRECTIONS:

PLEASE NOTE: BECAUSE THIS MATERIAL IS DESIGNED TO TEACH *AUDITORY* SEQUENTIAL MEMORY, THE STUDENT SHOULD NOT BE PERMITTED TO VIEW ANY OF THE NUMBERS, LETTERS OR WORDS IN THIS INSTUCTIONAL WORKBOOK AT ANY TIME.

There are three aspects of auditory sequential memory in this workbook. They are *numbers, letters* and *words*. The number, letter or word span (number of items in each series) is found in the table of contents *and* at the top of each page of the workbook. The instructor should present all *three* aspects at each session, allowing 3-5 minutes of instruction for each aspect. For remedial purposes, it is best to work with students at least two to three times a week on the development of these skills.

Finding the student's instructional level:

Begin by reading aloud the first number in the first exercise, Level I A (page 1), under ONE DIGIT NUMBER. If the student can recall the number after the first reading, the instructor moves on to the next single digit number. If the student can recall this number after the first reading, the next single digit number is presented. Once the student demonstrates that he can remember three consecutive single digit numbers after the first oral presentation, the instructor moves on to the TWO, SINGLE DIGIT NUMBERS series, Level 2 A (page3). The instructor continues to work with the student in the same manner in this level and the following levels until the instructional level of the student is determined, that is, until he or she is *unable* to recall the orally presented series after the first reading. That will be the student's instructional level. The same procedure should be used with letters and words.

Working on the exercise:

Begin working with the student at his instructional level as determined above. If the student is unable to recall the series correctly after the numbers, letters or words have been orally presented, the instructor repeats the same series again, without giving the student any clues, until the student responds correctly. Work in this manner encouraging the student to accurately repeat each new series after the first oral presentation.

As noted earlier, it is easier to hold a series of numbers, letters, or words in our minds if we group the series into smaller segments. Once a series reaches the five numbers, letter or word span level, it is best to present the series orally with a *slight pause* after each segment. Please note that *(slp)* is printed on the instruction pages to indicate where a *slight pause* should be made.

AUDITORY SEQUENTIAL MEMORY INSTRUCTIONAL WORKBOOK

Scoring and record keeping:

Record keeping helps the instructor to determine how far along in the workbook the student has progressed. Explain to your student that you will be keeping a record of his responses. As you work with him encourage him to improve his own score.

If the student is able to correctly repeat the series of numbers, letters or words that is orally presented after the first reading, he is given a presentation number of 1 on the *Auditory Sequential Memory Record Sheet,* under the *Presentation* column. A number of 1 is worth 100 points. If the student is unable to recall a series correctly after the first reading and it must be presented again, he receives a presentation number of 2, worth 50 points, for that series. If the instructor must read the series a third time before the student can recall the series correctly, the student is given a 3 with a value of zero. The object is for the student to consistently obtain three consecutive 1's (300 points) so that he can be moved into the next series level.

Sample of Scored Record Sheet

Score Total Key:

Presentation 1 = 100 points
Presentation 2 = 50 points
Presentation 3 = 0 points

Date	Level	N=Numbers L=Letters W=Words	Span (number of items in series)	1, 2, or 3 Presentations	Completed To: Page Number	Completed To: Item Number	Score Total
11/2/05	1 A	N	1	2,1,1,1,	1	4	350
11/6/05	2 A	N	2	1,2,2,1,3,	3	5	300

Continue at the student's instructional level until the student is able to easily recall a series of numbers at that level. Once he has mastered that series level, that is, obtains a score of three consecutive 1's, he can be moved into the next series level. Continue in this manner with numbers, letters, and words.

NOTE: Students are often motivated to perform better if they keep their own score card. They can draw a score card, as shown below, making a check mark under 100 for each series they recite correctly on the first try, under the 50 if they must have it repeated once, and under the 0 if they must have it presented more than twice.

Student Score Card

100	50	0

Results:

Once a student begins to develop his auditory sequential memory of numbers, letters and words, there will be a noticeable improvement in the student's ability to attend, listen and recall a series in all subject areas.

AUDITORY SEQUENTIAL MEMORY INSTRUCTIONAL WORKBOOK

*Directions: Please see detailed instructions on page iii.

ONE DIGIT NUMBER

SERIES-Level 1 A

NO.	
1.	6
2.	3
3.	1
4.	8
5.	9
6.	4
7.	7
8.	2
9.	0
10.	6
11.	1
12.	4
13.	8
14.	2
15.	0
16.	9
17.	3
18.	5
19.	6
20.	7

ONE DIGIT NUMBER

SERIES-Level 1 B

NO.	
1.	5
2.	8
3.	7
4.	2
5.	0
6.	1
7.	9
8.	4
9.	6
10.	3
11.	5
12.	2
13.	7
14.	8
15.	0
16.	1
17.	9
18.	5
19.	2
20.	6

AUDITORY SEQUENTIAL MEMORY INSTRUCTIONAL WORKBOOK

TWO, SINGLE DIGIT NUMBERS

SERIES-Level 2 A

NO.		
1.	1	2
2.	2	4
3.	6	5
4.	9	3
5.	8	6
6.	9	1
7.	4	8
8.	6	2
9.	1	7
10.	7	5
11.	4	9
12.	7	8
13.	6	2
14.	4	9
15.	7	2
16.	9	4
17.	4	6
18.	3	7
19.	2	8
20.	1	3

TWO, SINGLE DIGIT NUMBERS

SERIES-Level 2 B

NO.		
1.	8	1
2.	3	7
3.	2	4
4.	1	6
5.	9	0
6.	5	8
7.	4	1
8.	0	6
9.	8	3
10.	3	7
11.	6	1
12.	9	9
13.	5	2
14.	1	3
15.	8	0
16.	4	6
17.	1	9
18.	3	5
19.	2	1
20.	7	4

THREE, SINGLE DIGIT NUMBERS

SERIES-Level 3 A

NO.			
1.	1	3	5
2.	8	3	2
3.	9	5	6
4.	8	6	3
5.	9	8	6
6.	7	9	2
7.	3	1	4
8.	7	5	3
9.	2	8	9
10.	7	1	7
11.	5	9	8
12.	5	5	3
13.	9	1	6
14.	2	8	4
15.	3	7	1
16.	5	9	4
17.	8	8	5
18.	6	3	1
19.	4	1	2
20.	4	7	0

THREE, SINGLE DIGIT NUMBERS

SERIES-Level 3 B

NO.			
1.	6	2	9
2.	1	8	3
3.	5	4	2
4.	9	7	9
5.	2	4	5
6.	1	6	3
7.	4	0	2
8.	5	8	5
9.	3	0	1
10.	2	4	3
11.	6	5	2
12.	9	0	4
13.	7	3	9
14.	3	2	0
15.	4	4	9
16.	0	3	6
17.	7	3	0
18.	2	9	7
19.	8	3	8
20.	1	9	0

FOUR, SINGLE DIGIT NUMBERS

SERIES-Level 4 A

NO.				
1.	1	8	6	9
2.	3	5	2	7
3.	6	8	7	5
4.	9	3	4	2
5.	7	3	1	9
6.	8	9	7	2
7.	6	5	3	6
8.	7	1	9	3
9.	6	2	5	8
10.	9	3	4	1
11.	8	1	1	7
12.	6	2	9	9
13.	8	3	5	1
14.	4	2	1	5
15.	3	2	8	9
16.	2	7	1	4
17.	5	3	9	6
18.	2	4	1	6
19.	6	7	5	9
20.	5	3	9	7

FOUR, SINGLE DIGIT NUMBERS

SERIES-Level 4 B

NO.				
1.	4	3	7	4
2.	2	5	0	0
3.	1	9	3	4
4.	7	2	6	8
5.	2	7	4	1
6.	8	6	1	3
7.	5	7	2	9
8.	4	1	3	5
9.	9	2	1	9
10.	2	2	8	7
11.	6	4	3	9
12.	5	1	8	8
13.	3	3	9	0
14.	8	2	2	8
15.	4	6	0	1
16.	1	7	4	6
17.	7	5	5	2
18.	0	9	6	4
19.	6	4	7	3
20.	2	8	1	5

FIVE, SINGLE DIGIT NUMBERS (*slp*) =slight pause

SERIES-Level 5 A

NO.					
1.	2	8 (*slp*)	7	5	3
2.	4	7 (*slp*)	9	2	1
3.	3	3 (*slp*)	6	8	2
4.	9	2 (*slp*)	8	9	4
5.	3	6 (slp)	7	5	6
6.	8	7 (slp)	1	4	5
7.	8	5 (slp)	1	9	2
8.	3	4 (slp)	0	2	4
9.	6	8 (slp)	9	7	2
10.	5	1 (slp)	4	3	6
11.	3	7 (slp)	5	5	*3*
12.	4	2 (slp)	3	7	1
13.	6	1 (slp)	9	0	2
14.	2	7 (slp)	8	5	7
15.	1	9 (slp)	3	2	8
16.	6	4 (slp)	4	7	9
17.	5	3 (slp)	2	0	1
18.	9	7 (slp)	8	9	9
19.	5	5 (slp)	1	7	5
20.	7	8 (slp)	0	9	8

FIVE, SINGLE DIGIT NUMBERS (*slp*) =slight pause

SERIES-Level 5 B

NO.					
1.	2	5 (slp)	8	4	0
2.	2	1 (slp)	7	3	6
3.	7	2 (slp)	6	8	3
4.	8	3 (slp)	4	9	4
5.	1	6 (slp)	3	3	6
6.	9	4 (slp)	4	7	7
7.	3	5 (slp)	9	2	9
8.	5	9 (slp)	1	5	5
9.	0	7 (slp)	8	6	2
10.	4	8 (slp)	6	1	1
11.	7	2 (slp)	7	4	4
12.	6	3 (slp)	5	8	3
13.	2	1 (slp)	2	9	1
14.	8	5 (slp)	3	2	8
15.	3	6 (slp)	4	0	9
16.	1	9 (slp)	1	7	6
17.	5	4 (slp)	9	3	7
18.	2	6 (slp)	1	8	4
19.	9	9 (slp)	2	6	5
20.	1	0 (slp)	3	5	9

SIX, SINGLE DIGIT NUMBERS (*slp*) =slight pause

SERIES-Level 6 A

NO.						
1.	3	9	0 (slp)	5	3	2
2.	1	4	7 (slp)	3	5	8
3.	8	3	9 (slp)	2	7	4
4.	3	9	1 (slp)	4	2	6
5.	6	2	5 (slp)	9	6	7
6.	9	1	3 (slp)	8	8	1
7.	2	8	4 (slp)	1	1	9
8.	5	5	2 (slp)	6	4	5
9.	7	0	6 (slp)	7	9	3
10.	4	2	8 (slp)	0	0	2
11.	3	3	9 (slp)	4	5	4
12.	1	4	1 (slp)	3	2	8
13.	6	5	0 (slp)	2	3	6
14.	8	9	7 (slp)	5	7	0
15.	9	7	5 (slp)	9	6	7
16.	2	5	4 (slp)	8	8	1
17.	3	8	3 (slp)	1	5	9
18.	5	1	6 (slp)	7	1	5
19.	0	2	2 (slp)	3	9	3
20.	7	7	8 (slp)	4	2	0

SIX, SINGLE DIGIT NUMBERS (*slp*) =slight pause

SERIES-Level 6 B

NO.						
1.	2	7	4 (slp)	7	9	3
2.	4	1	0 (slp)	7	3	2
3.	2	6	3 (slp)	5	1	0
4.	2	8	2 (slp)	4	7	1
5.	5	2	9 (slp)	3	0	4
6.	8	9	7 (slp)	1	6	5
7.	7	5	5 (slp)	2	8	7
8.	1	4	1 (slp)	6	5	8
9.	3	3	6 (slp)	8	2	6
10.	6	7	4 (slp)	9	4	9
11.	0	0	8 (slp)	7	9	2
12.	2	1	0 (slp)	5	3	3
13.	4	6	2 (slp)	4	1	1
14.	5	2	3 (slp)	0	7	8
15.	0	9	9 (slp)	3	2	4
16.	9	8	1 (slp)	2	5	6
17.	3	5	4 (slp)	1	8	5
18.	7	7	3 (slp)	0	1	8
19.	5	9	2 (slp)	9	0	4
20.	6	2	7 (slp)	3	8	0

SEVEN, SINGLE DIGIT NUMBERS (*slp*) =slight pause

SERIES-Level 7 A

NO.							
1.	8	4	5 (slp)	9	0	3	2
2.	7	2	6 (slp)	0	1	4	4
3.	8	1	9 (slp)	6	7	0	2
4.	5	8	2 (slp)	5	1	3	9
5.	2	8	4 (slp)	7	3	0	4
6.	3	6	8 (slp)	3	4	8	6
7.	2	1	6 (slp)	3	5	4	1
8.	8	0	1 (slp)	2	4	3	8
9.	2	1	5 (slp)	7	9	0	4
10.	6	3	9 (slp)	5	1	0	3
11.	7	9	8 (slp)	2	4	7	5
12.	8	3	4 (slp)	5	9	6	1
13.	5	2	7 (slp)	4	8	2	1
14.	8	3	4 (slp)	2	1	0	5
15.	5	4	3 (slp)	7	5	1	9
16.	9	2	1 (slp)	5	3	7	2
17.	7	3	2 (slp)	8	4	1	0
18.	7	4	2 (slp)	8	5	4	0
19.	2	7	5 (slp)	9	1	6	7
20.	3	2	6 (slp)	5	5	1	8

SEVEN, SINGLE DIGIT NUMBERS (*slp*) =slight pause

SERIES-Level 7 B

NO.							
1.	4	8	3 (slp)	0	1	2	7
2.	0	2	5 (slp)	2	0	9	4
3.	7	3	4 (slp)	1	3	9	5
4.	6	2	3 (slp)	7	4	8	3
5.	2	3	8 (slp)	9	1	3	9
6.	8	0	2 (slp)	3	5	1	4
7.	6	2	3 (slp)	1	9	7	2
8.	1	4	9 (slp)	3	0	2	8
9.	7	7	1 (slp)	4	6	5	6
10.	3	5	0 (slp)	8	2	6	7
11.	4	2	8 (slp)	6	7	4	0
12.	8	1	4 (slp)	2	8	0	1
13.	2	8	5 (slp)	5	3	1	4
14.	0	6	6 (slp)	0	6	2	4
15.	5	3	7 (slp)	9	4	8	3
16.	9	9	1 (slp)	7	1	9	5
17.	3	0	2 (slp)	2	5	3	0
18.	1	8	3 (slp)	8	0	4	6
19.	7	2	9 (slp)	3	9	6	7
20.	9	3	5 (slp)	1	8	7	3

ONE, TWO DIGIT NUMBER

SERIES-Level 1 A

NO.	
1.	31
2.	18
3.	26
4.	15
5.	37
6.	48
7.	55
8.	19
9.	33
10.	14
11.	46
12.	27
13.	12
14.	53
15.	42
16.	29
17.	15
18.	35
19.	26
20.	10

ONE, TWO DIGIT NUMBER

SERIES-Level 1 B

NO.	
1.	68
2.	94
3.	72
4.	67
5.	90
6.	85
7.	99
8.	63
9.	88
10.	70
11.	97
12.	86
13.	75
14.	61
15.	83
16.	60
17.	77
18.	91
19.	63
20.	82

PROGRESSIVE TRAINING FOR TWO, TWO DIGIT NUMBERS

SERIES-Level 2 A

NO.		
1.	10	5
2.	15	1
3.	39	4
4.	88	3
5.	63	2
6.	58	5
7.	33	6
8.	85	8
9.	27	0
10.	42	7
11.	55	2
12.	97	6
13.	58	2
14.	86	3
15.	22	8
16.	90	6
17.	47	4
18.	53	2
19.	67	7
20.	62	1

TWO, TWO DIGIT NUMBERS

SERIES-Level 2 B

NO.		
1.	10	12
2.	39	13
3.	15	18
4.	20	25
5.	13	86
6.	72	63
7.	80	97
8.	26	35
9.	60	37
10.	52	83
11.	63	39
12.	24	22
13.	98	96
14.	88	65
15.	70	55
16.	52	85
17.	11	36
18	51	97
19.	61	52
20.	43	39

PROGRESSIVE TRAINING FOR THREE, TWO DIGIT NUMBERS

SERIES-Level 3 A

NO.			
1.	38	49	3
2.	18	48	8
3.	53	26	6
4.	28	33	4
5.	58	52	9
6.	38	18	1
7.	61	25`	7
8.	34	81	5
9.	70	46	9
10.	10	37	2
11.	63	33	9
12.	83	40	1
13.	49	36	3
14.	77	29	4
15.	25	13	6
16.	23	74	5
17.	76	31	7
18.	88	45	8
19.	62	22	2
20.	67	25	9

THREE, TWO DIGIT NUMBERS

SERIES-Level 3 B

NO.			
1.	12	14	36
2.	19	36	52
3.	25	30	27
4.	85	62	79
5.	93	37	27
6.	82	16	39
7.	73	75	22
8.	19	98	34
9.	77	14	67
10.	61	81	55
11.	29	15	84
12.	49	35	14
13.	90	24	68
14.	72	28	51
15.	80	38	72
16.	44	94	36
17.	52	21	14
18.	47	36	33
19.	37	27	99
20.	50	65	39

ONE, THREE DIGIT NUMBER

SERIES-Level 1 A

NO.	
1.	358
2.	431
3.	348
4.	258
5.	358
6.	269
7.	136
8.	316
9.	326
10.	179
11.	505
12.	327
13.	431
14.	545
15.	186
16.	332
17.	182
18.	228
19.	219
20.	102

ONE, THREE DIGIT NUMBER

SERIES-Level 1 B

NO.	
1.	796
2.	995
3.	704
4.	824
5.	601
6.	889
7.	623
8.	805
9.	775
10.	970
11.	707
12.	761
13.	698
14.	615
15.	952
16.	737
17.	709
18.	678
19.	809
20.	763

PROGRESSIVE TRAINING FOR TWO, THREE DIGIT NUMBERS

SERIES-Level 2 A

NO.		
1.	292	2
2.	593	1
3.	852	5
4.	777	9
5.	523	4
6.	846	6
7.	242	7
8.	319	8
9.	688	3
10.	719	2
11.	577	1
12.	259	4
13.	538	9
14.	138	2
15.	338	0
16.	835	8
17.	523	5
18.	356	6
19.	940	7
20.	774	3

PROGRESSIVE TRAINING FOR TWO, THREE DIGIT NUMBERS

SERIES-Level 2B

NO.		
1.	846	45
2.	573	53
3.	973	27
4.	318	46
5.	245	99
6.	178	74
7.	222	86
8.	156	75
9.	757	23
10.	359	22
11.	570	36
12.	284	45
13.	921	78
14.	347	44
15.	258	99
16.	472	51
17.	328	22
18.	759	11
19.	339	75
20.	156	57

TWO, THREE DIGIT NUMBERS

SERIES-Level 2 C

NO.		
1.	321	619
2.	368	205
3.	259	150
4.	160	820
5.	295	173
6.	381	206
7.	881	193
8.	943	638
9.	194	377
10.	249	334
11.	613	294
12.	127	268
13.	924	189
14.	223	545
15.	593	129
16.	231	977
17.	244	293
18.	367	721
19.	572	605
20.	236	836

PROGRESSIVE TRAINING FOR THREE, THREE DIGIT NUMBERS

SERIES-Level 3 A

NO.			
1.	738	295	2
2.	593	159	1
3.	247	251	5
4.	246	422	7
5.	101	721	4
6.	128	372	6
7.	931	394	1
8.	288	301	3
9.	469	336	2
10.	987	249	7
11.	638	325	9
12.	247	839	3
13.	886	347	8
14.	231	674	5
15.	356	733	0
16.	358	352	1
17.	326	388	8
18.	859	471	2
19.	743	897	4
20.	859	939	7

PROGRESSIVE TRAINING FOR THREE, THREE DIGIT NUMBERS

SERIES-Level 3 B

NO.			
1.	835	346	21
2.	768	315	74
3.	527	739	44
4.	843	651	83
5.	385	294	36
6.	947	204	67
7.	552	375	90
8.	269	294	71
9.	436	158	37
10.	336	254	10
11.	843	394	55
12.	216	351	36
13.	685	374	78
14.	446	881	15
15.	231	638	49
16.	378	484	83
17.	455	130	71
18.	587	209	62
19.	638	529	44
20.	117	749	27

THREE, THREE DIGIT NUMBERS

SERIES-Level 3 C

NO.			
1.	436	830	140
2.	748	565	573
3.	137	840	359
4.	537	843	903
5.	325	714	862
6.	830	271	265
7.	345	738	962
8.	127	361	789
9.	884	347	293
10.	772	433	278
11.	336	261	945
12.	735	823	316
13.	601	237	231
14.	341	583	703
15.	226	391	238
16.	735	197	337
17.	448	236	184
18.	157	372	288
19.	651	348	241
20.	237	131	172

ONE LETTER SERIES

SERIES-Level 1 A

NO.	
1.	A
2.	B
3.	T
4.	Q
5.	V
6.	N
7.	W
8.	M
9.	X
10.	P
11.	Z
12.	O
13.	C
14.	I
15.	J
16.	K
17.	L
18.	D
19.	H
20.	S

ONE LETTER SERIES

SERIES-Level 1 B

NO.	
1.	W
2.	U
3.	Z
4.	O
5.	M
6.	C
7.	X
8.	E
9.	Q
10.	P
11.	A
12.	I
13.	K
14.	L
15.	U
16.	D
17.	T
18.	S
19.	V
20.	J

TWO LETTER SERIES

SERIES-Level 2 A

NO.		
1.	L	E
2.	A	F
3.	Z	I
4.	O	G
5.	E	F
6.	H	O
7.	U	M
8.	P	L
9.	B	U
10.	N	A
11.	V	A
12.	U	G
13.	A	B
14.	U	X
15.	Z	I
16.	E	C
17.	H	A
18.	I	J
19.	M	O
20.	K	E

TWO LETTER SERIES

SERIES-Level 2 B

NO.		
1.	D	B
2.	X	Z
3.	C	R
4.	Q	L
5.	V	B
6.	T	W
7.	Q	K
8.	B	X
9.	H	G
10.	S	W
11.	R	U
12.	P	F
13.	J	R
14.	Y	X
15.	M	Q
16.	X	T
17.	A	E
18.	D	H
19.	G	N
20.	L	D

THREE LETTER SERIES

SERIES-Level 3 A

NO.			
1.	B	I	R
2.	W	E	M
3.	Y	O	P
4.	D	A	K
5.	B	I	X
6.	R	U	C
7.	T	E	M
8.	M	I	V
9.	Q	E	C
10.	F	O	B
11.	V	U	X
12.	S	A	V
13.	J	I	B
14.	L	U	C
15.	X	E	N
16.	D	I	W
17.	G	E	S
18.	T	O	K
19.	Y	E	Z
20.	Q	O	F

THREE LETTER SERIES

SERIES-Level 3 B

NO.			
1.	A	Z	B
2.	B	C	K
3.	X	Z	Y
4.	M	P	O
5.	W	U	E
6.	X	R	O
7.	G	F	N
8.	K	H	V
9.	D	F	S
10.	Y	L	G
11.	Z	N	J
12.	V	S	Q
13.	I	M	R
14.	C	O	F
15.	D	W	A
16.	U	T	H
17.	B	N	Y
18.	J	L	W
19.	Q	T	K
20.	U	X	B

AUDITORY SEQUENTIAL MEMORY INSTRUCTIONAL WORKBOOK

FOUR LETTER SERIES

SERIES-Level 4 A

NO.				
1.	T	E	L	P
2.	C	E	M	E
3.	W	R	I	N
4.	Q	U	E	M
5.	Z	O	K	E
6.	R	O	F	T
7.	G	E	N	D
8.	D	A	R	P
9.	K	O	A	B
10.	S	O	I	X
11.	H	A	G	H
12.	J	O	E	M
13.	Y	O	U	X
14.	W	E	V	S
15.	S	P	A	K
16.	T	R	E	L
17.	Z	O	O	F
18.	H	I	L	E
19.	P	R	A	B
20.	B	L	A	Y

FOUR LETTER SERIES

SERIES-Level 4 B

NO.				
1.	A	Z	P	T
2.	Z	K	H	O
3.	R	Y	Z	T
4.	A	O	P	G
5.	N	I	B	R
6.	R	M	F	J
7.	L	N	S	V
8.	W	U	O	Z
9.	Y	P	U	C
10.	X	D	B	M
11.	G	Z	Q	T
12.	H	F	S	P
13.	Y	V	S	O
14.	F	L	I	R
15.	D	W	Y	J
16.	C	B	P	H
17.	Z	X	M	E
18.	N	P	R	H
19.	G	O	L	Q
20.	X	B	U	V

AUDITORY SEQUENTIAL MEMORY INSTRUCTIONAL WORKBOOK

FIVE LETTER SERIES (*slp*) =slight pause

SERIES-Level 5 A

NO.					
1.	T	R (slp)	O	M	E
2.	C	L (slp)	A	C	K
3.	Y	O (slp)	H	E	D
4.	Q	U (slp)	O	A	F
5.	Z	E (slp)	R	E	T
6.	S	P (slp)	L	A	D
7.	R	O (slp)	A	K	E
8.	W	R (slp)	E	N	G
9.	S	T (slp)	R	O	M
10.	F	R (slp)	O	A	B
11.	T	E slp)	E	D	E
12.	B	L (slp)	A	F	E
13.	F	O (slp)	O	G	H
14.	V	E (slp)	N	C	E
15.	A	D (slp)	D	L	E
16.	J	A (slp)	U	P	E
17.	C	R (slp)	I	B	E
18.	T	U (slp)	D	E	R
19.	P	R (slp)	I	E	L
20.	B	E (slp)	N	O	P

FIVE LETTER SERIES (*slp*) =slight pause

SERIES-Level 5 B

NO.					
1.	X	T *(slp)*	V	R	Z
2.	Y	O *(slp)*	M	G	Q
3.	X	Z *(slp)*	A	B	Y
4.	W	Y *(slp)*	E	A	P
5.	M	R *(slp)*	Y	V	W
6.	P	X *(slp)*	Z	C	D
7.	K	L *(slp)*	E	U	R
8.	V	W *(slp)*	Z	E	I
9.	Q	T *(slp)*	B	Y	N
10.	F	H *(slp)*	O	J	S
11.	Z	U (slp)	H	C	M
12.	T	B *(slp)*	W	Y	Q
13.	X	R *(slp)*	N	E	Z
14.	S	A *(slp)*	K	B	W
15.	H	I *(slp)*	X	W	A
16.	P	R *(slp)*	V	C	M
17.	G	S *(slp)*	B	X	Z
18.	D	V *(slp)*	P	Q	R
19.	J	D *(slp)*	K	I	Y
20.	U	W *(slp)*	Z	L	R

AUDITORY SEQUENTIAL MEMORY INSTRUCTIONAL WORKBOOK

SIX LETTER SERIES (*slp*) =slight pause

SERIES-Level 6 A

NO.						
1.	W	E	N (slp)	T	I	R
2.	D	R	O (slp)	O	M	S
3.	Y	E	T (slp)	P	E	N
4.	Q	U	O (slp)	P	E	D
5.	S	T	R (slp)	E	E	B
6.	Z	O	O (slp)	K	L	E
7.	B	L	A (slp)	Y	E	D
8.	N	E	M (slp)	M	E	T
9.	F	R	E (slp)	E	T	S
10.	M	U	D (slp)	T	I	N
11.	P	L	I (slp)	E	V	E
12.	F	R	O (slp)	U	P	S
13.	R	E	G (slp)	H	A	N
14.	W	R	A (slp)	Y	E	D
15.	P	E	T (slp)	I	O	N
16.	C	L	E (slp)	K	E	T
17.	T	E	X (slp)	I	N	G
18.	S	P	L (slp)	O	R	E
19.	J	O	I (slp)	K	L	E
20.	R	A	S (slp)	M	I	C

SIX LETTER SERIES (*slp*) =slight pause

SERIES-Level 6 B

NO.						
1.	F	W	H (slp)	I	K	P
2.	D	V	N (slp)	Q	Z	R
3.	Y	P	L (slp)	C	N	M
4.	C	X	B (slp)	J	P	W
5.	Q	S	T (slp)	K	R	B
6.	R	F	G (slp)	H	W	V
7.	D	T	Y (slp)	J	W	M
8.	W	B	R (slp)	C	E	D
9.	I	U	T (slp)	M	W	P
10.	L	C	A (slp)	Q	W	J
11.	X	Z	O (slp)	E	S	S
12.	N	W	S (slp)	K	L	B
13.	D	W	Y (slp)	X	Z	Q
14.	G	G	R (slp)	W	P	I
15.	A	D	E (slp)	Y	F	Y
16.	O	C	F (slp)	W	X	M
17.	J	B	W (slp)	Q	K	L
18.	H	R	A (slp)	Q	F	T
19.	M	V	Z (slp)	Y	U	W
20.	W	L	S (slp)	G	K	P

SEVEN LETTER SERIES (*slp*) =slight pause

SERIES-Level 7 A

NO.							
1.	S	T	R (slp)	A	I	G	H
2.	P	R	O (slp)	G	L	E	S
3.	D	R	E (slp)	E	T	E	R
4.	S	P	A (slp)	Y	I	S	H
5.	B	L	R (slp)	O	V	E	S
6.	Y	O	I (slp)	Z	E	T	S
7.	S	M	A (slp)	E	V	E	N
8.	J	E	K (slp)	E	R	Y	S
9.	C	L	O (slp)	W	O	R	Y
10.	Q	U	E (slp)	F	F	E	R
11.	L	A	C (slp)	T	I	N	G
12.	T	R	E (slp)	W	O	C	S
13.	V	I	B (slp)	B	E	R	Y
14.	F	L	O (slp)	M	E	T	S
15.	D	R	E (slp)	E	T	O	N
16.	N	A	M (slp)	L	E	R	T
17.	B	I	X (slp)	R	O	U	N
18.	H	E	G (slp)	G	E	R	T
19.	Z	E	B (slp)	B	E	S	S
20.	K	L	U (slp)	M	F	E	D

SEVEN LETTER SERIES (*slp*) =slight pause

SERIES-Level 7 B

NO.							
1.	Y	A	R (slp)	T	L	E	Y
2.	W	A	U (slp)	L	I	N	G
3.	F	R	A (slp)	P	P	E	R
4.	J	O	V (slp)	E	E	N	S
5.	W	R	I (slp)	D	G	O	Y
6.	Q	U	A (slp)	Y	I	N	G
7.	S	T	R (slp)	E	V	E	T
8.	Z	A	M (slp)	P	O	I	T
9.	T	R	U (slp)	V	F	E	N
10.	P	L	R (slp)	E	W	O	T
11.	B	L	O (slp)	A	V	E	D
12.	Y	O	D (slp)	Z	E	L	S
13.	W	R	A (slp)	N	T	E	R
14.	K	L	R (slp)	I	M	I	T
15.	C	R	I (slp)	D	A	S	H
16.	V	O	L (slp)	E	R	I	G
17.	L	A	U (slp)	T	E	R	N
18.	Y	U	P (slp)	P	A	N	Y
19.	Z	I	T (slp)	H	E	S	T
20.	H	A	S (slp)	H	P	O	P

ONE, ONE SYLLABLE WORD

SERIES-Level 1 A

NO.	
1.	hat
2.	look
3.	was
4.	boy
5.	run
6.	saw
7.	is
8.	she
9.	cat
10.	he
11.	can
12.	the
13.	ran
14.	dog
15.	toy
16.	go
17.	at
18.	said
19.	all
20.	went

ONE, ONE SYLLABLE WORD

SERIES-Level 1 B

NO.	
1.	gate
2.	train
3.	dish
4.	kite
5.	street
6.	batch
7.	smell
8.	jump
9.	fence
10.	main
11.	crown
12.	fence
13.	house
14.	brain
15.	treat
16.	yawn
17.	sleep
18.	dance
19.	laugh
20.	slide

TWO, ONE SYLLABLE WORDS

SERIES-Level 2 A

NO.		
1.	box	hat
2.	boat	sail
3.	house	door
4.	book	page
5.	sink	drain
6.	ball	bat
7.	dog	pet
8.	jar	jam
9.	star	sky
10.	beard	goat
11.	barn	pig
12.	doll	eyes
13.	face	clown
14.	train	track
15.	tree	leaf
16.	shirt	tie
17.	lace	shoe
18.	snow	ice
19.	dress	girl
20.	car	seat

TWO, ONE SYLLABLE WORDS

SERIES-Level 2 B

NO.		
1.	yard	car
2.	cup	pet
3.	treat	nose
4.	pig	ball
5.	train	walk
6.	rock	box
7.	line	truck
8.	hill	girl
9.	dance	rain
10.	house	doll
11.	dance	hop
12.	boat	see
13.	grass	trick
14.	rain	sand
15.	road	spoon
16.	cow	truck
17.	hair	jump
18.	coat	treat
19.	dirt	stair
20.	floor	pen

THREE, ONE SYLLABLE WORDS

SERIES-Level 3 A

NO.			
1.	lamb	corn	cap
2.	fence	house	lamp
3.	tree	school	milk
4.	pig	yard	shoe
5.	socks	clock	tie
6.	cow	lake	boat
7.	bat	street	porch
8.	sand	sled	cart
9.	pear	hands	train
10.	card	face	door
11.	toy	wet	run
12.	round	sit	fun
13.	tray	sock	fat
14.	home	warm	nice
15.	blue	sweet	hand
16.	ear	page	win
17.	go	cane	top
18.	swim	door	add
19.	fit	tall	desk
20.	wash	watch	paint

THREE, ONE SYLLABLE WORDS

SERIES-Level 3 B

NO.			
1.	pup	come	queen
2.	box	zoo	ring
3.	wash	scream	free
4.	drain	flat	rent
5.	pop	swim	gray
6.	week	write	line
7.	sent	live	like
8.	sweet	crane	dirt
9.	shut	brush	jam
10.	fly	flip	barn
11.	duck	light	clock
12.	crawl	blue	grow
13.	slim	wide	high
14.	desk	plate	shine
15.	gray	drive	smooth
16.	white	leaf	worm
17.	catch	kick	yard
18.	fix	watch	spell
19.	stay	sew	cloth
20.	plow	rows	green

FOUR, ONE SYLLABLE WORDS

SERIES-Level 4 A.

NO.				
1.	couch	boy	hat	bat
2.	grass	board	blue	jug
3.	rain	mud	shoe	map
4.	lace	store	girl	school
5.	dress	suit	park	tree
6.	light	chair	mouse	top
7.	bulb	come	dirt	bag
8.	pin	toe	foot	rod
9.	pet	cat	track	zoo
10.	floor	soap	cloth	mop
11.	joy	smart	day	duck
12.	book	close	month	clock
13.	crawl	write	glass	rug
14.	red	stair	thin	door
15.	was	take	yard	now
16.	couch	shelf	clothes	play
17.	track	ring	fall	bead
18.	ear	trunk	wood	squirt
19.	learn	nose	lamp	train
20.	corn	tap	eat	dish

FOUR, ONE SYLLABLE WORDS

SERIES-Level 4 B

NO.				
1.	type	glass	storm	snow
2.	screen	hair	frame	fins
3.	cord	tone	nine	blocks
4.	squint	roads	sign	round
5.	robe	paint	shirt	sewn
6.	ride	squeak	roof	trim
7.	grin	cute	school	gym
8.	bounce	stones	hill	beam
9.	beak	bird	long	spin
10.	bright	stars	streak	edge
11.	moon	glow	height	falls
12.	twin	jumps	board	split
13.	trace	scene	sheet	trees
14.	nest	wren	twigs	cat
15.	pins	bowl	lawn	throw
16.	win	cheer	lane	race
17.	fish	nice	line	catch
18.	legs	beach	room	float
19.	waves	glide	tide	bridge
20.	bill	reach	paid	taste

AUDITORY SEQUENTIAL MEMORY INSTRUCTIONAL WORKBOOK

FIVE, ONE SYLLABLE WORDS (slp) =slight pause

SERIES-Level 5 A

NO.					
1.	sled	lake (slp)	ice	snow	hat
2.	pear	hands (slp)	gloves	door	milk
3.	tree	school (slp)	brick	boy	clock
4.	bat	plant (slp)	cow	worm	dirt
5.	fair	hair (slp)	book	write	desk
6.	stool	bowl (slp)	dish	spoon	tree
7.	rug	paint (slp)	brush	tie	string
8.	line	trip (slp)	watch	can	find
9.	bird	seed (slp)	bell	house	lawn
10.	drink	peach (slp)	boy	shirt	camp
11.	skip	plant (slp)	now	brain	pup
12.	fun	shine (slp)	skip	cow	train
13.	bean	sew (slp)	rat	line	scarf
14.	glove	throw (slp)	net	man	fish
15.	page	shut (slp)	turn	cot	light
16.	turn	night (slp)	fade	star	top
17.	arm	soft (slp)	fork	sing	trace
18.	flag	yell (slp)	blue	fat	soon
19.	roof	slide (slp)	boot	rake	bud
20.	draw	white (slp)	fan	place	lock

FIVE, ONE SYLLABLE WORDS (slp) =slight pause

SERIES-Level 5 B

NO.					
1.	tub	churn	cream (slp)	brook	swish
2.	hive	comb	stick (slp)	buzz	swarm
3.	pond	gold	swirl (slp)	split	torn
4.	jewel	shine	ring (slp)	break	buy
5.	teach	learn	smart (slp)	prize	win
6.	guest	porch	sink (slp)	wade	grain
7.	square	pegs	heart (slp)	crown	king
8.	flit	crane	swamp (slp)	legs	food
9.	quick	crib	doll (slp)	roll	hand
10.	dense	thick	wipe (slp)	fog	shine
11.	rest	sleep	need (slp)	good	time
12.	crop	crow	space (slp)	wind	corn
13.	burn	cool	fan (slp)	screen	health
14.	zoom	road	track (slp)	dust	hot
15.	mend	hole	patch (slp)	cloth	read
16.	camp	track	youth (slp)	dive	luck
17.	quit	start	high (slp)	score	work
18.	heart	kind	bloom (slp)	vine	ridge
19.	blend	swim	milk (slp)	strong	climb
20.	great	grin	smile (slp)	good	mind

SIX ONE SYLLABLE WORDS (slp) =slight pause

SERIES-Level 6 A

NO.						
1.	month	dates	tree (slp)	leaf	high	cane
2.	beard	man	walk (slp)	slow	vase	full
3.	sit	fly	vine (slp)	sway	time	old
4.	jet	sky	blue (slp)	wind	leave	shout
5.	door	knob	wood (slp)	gain	brown	step
6.	young	girl	nose (slp)	count	name	box
7.	knot	small	salt (slp)	lake	cave	weed
8.	crate	cork	pick (slp)	bean	skip	wet
9.	stem	ant	hole (slp)	lift	crumb	now
10.	logs	chop	good (slp)	true	wig	job
11.	work	fun	like (slp)	help	still	print
12.	curl	blush	rock (slp)	square	dress	waltz
13.	disk	clip	sheep (slp)	spring	jump	free
14.	black	red	car (slp)	wheel	pail	wish
15.	seed	plant	sharp (slp)	grate	side	grape
16.	sock	boot	horse (slp)	rein	leap	stake
17.	zoo	cage	seal (slp)	kind	laugh	squirt
18.	bus	deck	store (slp)	clerk	close	pout
19.	shell	sea	joy (slp)	sun	sleep	sound
20.	horn	blow	shine (slp)	loud	vase	smash

SIX ONE SYLLABLE WORDS (slp) =slight pause

SERIES-Level 6 B

NO.						
1.	sack	box	beans (slp)	mark	need	drain
2.	cove	cliff	waves (slp)	mine	gold	dig
3.	rash	hot	sick (slp)	cool	wet	heat
4.	weird	cow	spots (slp)	cud	sing	proud
5.	eyes	blink	gain (slp)	grades	beat	score
6.	fur	ice	smooth (slp)	warm	feet	skin
7.	clown	act	switch (slp)	clothes	feet	long
8.	frog	leap	croak (slp)	deep	voice	rain
9.	mouse	small	spin (slp)	peep	chick	scratch
10.	pet	dog	roll (slp)	fun	fur	fluff
11.	plop	quest	trail (slp)	land	west	find
12.	squaw	beads	sew (slp)	tan	hunt	bow
13.	switch	track	wind (slp)	work	hard	crews
14.	palm	gnats	sweat (slp)	haul	mule	boat
15.	shop	reign	king (slp)	vote	rocks	creek
16.	lift	weigh	load (slp)	pipe	wet	drink
17.	yeast	beast	lion (slp)	bread	eat	rise
18.	grab	sting	bugs (slp)	clang	swat	bring
19.	juice	drink	orange (slp)	oats	smash	stir
20.	squint	glare	shade (slp)	cove	splash	grin

ONE, TWO SYLLABLE WORD

SERIES-Level 1 A

NO.	
1.	brother
2.	many
3.	lady
4.	follow
5.	around
6.	started
7.	happy
8.	almost
9.	children
10.	open
11.	yellow
12.	seven
13.	wanted
14.	after
15.	because
16.	myself
17.	pretty
18.	only
19.	riding
20.	today

ONE, TWO SYLLABLE WORD

SERIES-Level 1 B

NO.	
1.	river
2.	ocean
3.	pencil
4.	fancy
5.	zebra
6.	silver
7.	number
8.	floating
9.	looking
10.	slipper
11.	silly
12.	faster
13.	jumping
14.	mother
15.	rabbit
16.	sister
17.	kettle
18.	sticky
19.	father
20.	baby

PROGRESSIVE TRAINING FOR TWO, TWO SYLLABLE WORDS

SERIES-Level 2 A

NO.		
1.	garden	desk
2.	flower	mud
3.	table	cloth
4.	cattle	bat
5.	water	cup
6.	rocket	laugh
7.	picture	truck
8.	mountain	rain
9.	window	run
10.	eagle	plant
11.	cradle	pan
12.	monkey	train
13.	hopping	tree
14.	pocket	horse
15.	rabbit	shoe
16.	butter	dish
17.	paper	hair
18.	baby	sock
19.	skater	lace
20.	reader	hand

TWO, TWO SYLLABLE WORDS

SERIES-Level 2 B

NO.		
1.	puddle	pocket
2.	motor	tractor
3.	always	apple
4.	bottle	children
5.	circus	cookie
6.	paper	fountain
7.	river	skater
8.	wagon	ribbon
9.	baby	kettle
10.	color	city
11.	machine	sitter
12.	talking	cover
13.	whisper	button
14.	winter	pencil
15.	wrapper	chicken
16.	listen	learning
17.	measure	figure
18.	wishing	feather
19.	sweeter	scooter
20.	laughing	neighbor

PROGRESSIVE TRAINING FOR THREE, TWO SYLLABLE WORDS

SERIES-Level 3 A

NO.			
1.	melon	apple	ran
2.	lemon	mirror	look
3.	chapter	music	page
4.	clover	candy	leaf
5.	total	marble	cave
6.	other	many	read
7.	penny	nickel	now
8.	raining	jumping	year
9.	mother	parent	girl
10.	hotter	fatter	box
11.	water	because	see
12.	began	hopping	tree
13.	balloon	garden	round
14.	sister	window	where
15.	watching	morning	place
16.	swimming	birthday	word
17.	follow	inside	year
18.	below	between	watch
19.	something	also	now
20.	flower	pretty	still

THREE, TWO SYLLABLE WORDS

SERIES-Level 3 B

NO.			
1.	broken	flatten	wrapper
2.	crying	sweeping	laughing
3.	study	battle	turtle
4.	future	thicken	writer
5.	happy	rancher	packing
6.	pencil	rattle	crayon
7.	broken	splashing	helper
8.	chicken	mirror	author
9.	soldier	captain	jumper
10.	buggy	bridle	rider
11.	walker	money	weather
12.	pretty	camel	dolly
13.	wonder	laughter	helping
14.	bringing	picnic	drawing
15.	yellow	cooking	table
16.	finding	basket	racer
17.	funny	making	grower
18.	tiger	whisper	planter
19.	squirrel	raccoon	tapping
20.	leader	trading	soccer

PROGRESSIVE TRAINING FOR FOUR, TWO SYLLABLE WORDS

SERIES-Level 4 A

NO.				
1.	cartoon	circle	simple	moon
2.	follow	letter	pretend	eye
3.	reader	monkey	number	shape
4.	hungry	among	puzzle	word
5.	answer	object	question	play
6.	slipper	button	closet	wheat
7.	student	teacher	practice	case
8.	correct	opened	polite	nice
9.	added	handle	circle	draw
10.	listen	pieces	appear	thought
11.	happy	cartoon	bottle	boat
12.	going	many	center	eat
13.	yellow	under	today	try
14.	open	thinking	before	tell
15.	away	helping	after	cold
16.	working	faster	carry	kind
17.	always	giving	cleaner	wish
18.	surprise	children	people	said
19.	cousin	movie	brother	came
20.	castle	baby	started	all

FOUR, TWO SYLLABLE WORDS

SERIES-Level 4 B

NO.				
1.	support	wishes	almost	above
2.	kitchen	standing	adverb	runner
3.	future	solving	title	smiling
4.	perform	expect	reason	final
5.	happy	fishing	sadly	soccer
6.	final	baker	painter	lawyer
7.	writer	reader	frowning	shadow
8.	skipping	leaping	lemon	wiser
9.	cutting	tracing	dancer	washing
10.	study	smarter	thinking	pages
11.	skating	running	better	around
12.	teaching	listen	pencil	picture
13.	sofa	rubber	letter	flower
14.	farmer	rocket	sprinkle	raining
15.	mountain	creature	jumping	rabbit
16.	writing	question	meadow	sunny
17.	busy	fatter	skipping	rolling
18.	water	faster	color	cabin
19.	cover	flatten	airplane	flying
20.	ocean	sailing	trainer	fishing

AUDITORY SEQUENTIAL MEMORY INSTRUCTIONAL WORKBOOK

PROGRESSIVE TRAINING FOR FIVE, TWO SYLLABLE OR COMPOUND WORDS (slp) =slight pause

SERIES-Level 5 A

NO.					
1.	cable	happy (slp)	racket	booklet	card
2.	tractor	pencil (slp)	artist	circus	tent
3.	reader	silly (slp)	story	printer	couch
4.	lacy	sweater (slp)	flower	tablet	snow
5.	healthy	typist (slp)	support	railing	grass
6.	picture	music (slp)	castle	ugly	treat
7.	rabbit	runner (slp)	tiger	ocean	hat
8.	doctor	magic (slp)	study	science	porch
9.	pocket	shutter (slp)	husband	window	lawn
10.	sandbox	swinging (slp)	ladder	shouting	slide
11.	beehive	buzzing (slp)	berry	honey	sting
12.	houseboat	water (slp)	sunny	fishing	rain
13.	winter	driver (slp)	snowman	ceiling	box
14.	birthday	singing (slp)	laughter	puzzle	cart
15.	liking	sailboat (slp)	racing	mailbox	put
16.	windmill	river (slp)	basket	grinding	shoe
17.	letter	joyful (slp)	super	holding	tall
18.	shoebox	leather (slp)	doorknob	buckle	rat
19.	pumpkin	picking (slp)	hollow	spooky	blue
20.	thunder	raining (slp)	stumble	hiding	house

FIVE, TWO SYLLABLE OR COMPOUND WORDS (slp)=slight pause

SERIES-Level 5 B

NO.					
1.	lemon	marble (slp)	market	empty	problem
2.	grateful	army (slp)	lately	biggest	western
3.	awake	mistake (slp)	snowflake	inside	sidewalk
4.	jacket	hockey (slp)	faded	letter	shapely
5.	spaceman	angry (slp)	graceful	clanging	number
6.	ankle	blanket (slp)	stronger	longest	songbook
7.	drawing	crawling (slp)	elbow	shelter	awful
8.	necktie	spotted (slp)	freckle	speckled	answer
9.	iceberg	advice (slp)	nicest	reason	chickens
10.	tickets	thicken (slp)	gravy	fluffy	nickel
11.	differ	lifted (slp)	fifty	winking	trinkets
12.	turkey	gobble (slp)	object	cobwebs	modern
13.	foggy	goggles (slp)	racing	subway	bubbles
14.	muffins	fluffy (slp)	crushing	bushes	mushrooms
15.	winning	batter (slp)	wedding	party	pleasant
16.	fanning	tadpoles (slp)	gladness	ladder	jungle
17.	winner	finish (slp)	perhaps	happened	landscape
18.	crackle	sandwich (slp)	grumble	correct	lumber
19.	habit	fabric (slp)	smashing	dragon	eyelash
20.	flashy	swishing (slp)	vanish	medals	midnight

PROGRESSIVE TRAINING FOR SIX, TWO SYLLABLE OR COMPOUND WORDS (slp) =slight pause

SERIES-Level 6 A

NO.						
1.	minute	tractor	laughter (slp)	typing	railroad	fine
2.	leather	cowboy	facet (slp)	thunder	rolling	shade
3.	voting	freeing	battle (slp)	courage	detail	glance
4.	present	recall	lightning (slp)	trader	necktie	boots
5.	perform	model	printed (slp)	order	between	words
6.	provide	sequence	skipping (slp)	helpful	later	long
7.	expand	global	classroom (slp)	program	subject	trace
8.	adopt	enlarge	focus (slp)	exist	enhance	need
9.	differ	begin	textbook (slp)	excel	practice	group
10.	gifted	enter	written (slp)	language	study	win
11.	therefore	instant	create (slp)	appear	sometimes	try
12.	increase	frequent	sudden (slp)	apply	honor	great
13.	adult	fender	become (slp)	training	approach	read
14.	covered	again	reuse (slp)	streetcar	feather	light
15.	always	extra	today (slp)	afraid	bravely	round
16.	ever	quickly	fleeing (slp)	evade	sharing	hunt
17.	trusting	houseboat	pleasing (slp)	matter	joyful	shore
18.	chewing	scrubbing	workbook (slp)	learning	express	close
19.	passage	involve	angle (slp)	concern	kindness	clues
20.	sharpen	skillful	absorb (slp)	smallest	smarter	ranch

SIX, TWO SYLLABLE OR COMPOUND WORDS (slp) =slight pause

SERIES-Level 6 B

NO.						
1.	excel	assist	inform (slp)	college	belief	include
2.	produce	center	above (slp)	progress	receive	honor
3.	prepare	exam	outline (slp)	answer	clearing	knowledge
4.	guidance	wonder	special (slp)	pleasant	station	include
5.	matter	correct	convince (slp)	reduce	compute	adding
6.	control	handle	listen (slp)	knapsack	truly	likeness
7.	explain	afford	picture (slp)	sometimes	chalkboard	vision
8.	reserve	observe	second (slp)	holding	reverse	problems
9.	gifted	reward	pinpoint (slp)	repeat	knowing	amaze
10.	feature	movie	gather (slp)	sidewalk	voyage	embark
11.	shipyard	sailing	monster (slp)	waving	courage	funny
12.	jungle	captain	wither (slp)	stomping	descend	faster
13.	queenly	stately	flowing (slp)	scrapbook	statue	design
14.	paper	machine	publish (slp)	tracing	flying	airline
15.	figure	action	zooming (slp)	value	lifting	cartoon
16.	kitchen	silver	soaking (slp)	anxious	factor	youthful
17.	miser	mixture	hauling (slp)	prancing	roadway	racing
18.	venture	admire	talent (slp)	ballet	waltzing	chatting
19.	manage	request	joking (slp)	invent	surprise	conquer
20.	smartest	bravest	honest (slp)	banquet	laughter	joyful

Publishers Permission:
*Purchasers of **Auditory Sequential Memory Instructional Workbook** may reproduce this record sheet for classroom use only. **No other part of the instructional workbook may be reproduced.***

AUDITORY SEQUENTIAL MEMORY INSTRUCTIONAL WORKBOOK
RECORD SHEET

Name _____

Date	Level	N=Numbers L=Letters W=Words	Span*	1, 2, or 3 Presentations*	Completed To: Page Number	Item Number	Score Total

*Span (number of items in series)
* 1, 2, or 3 Presentations Key:
- 1. Indicates correct reciting after first presentation
- 2. Indicates correct reciting after a needed second presentation
- 3. Indicates more than two presentations required

Score Card

100	50	0

Score Card: Students are often motivated to perform better if they can keep their own score card. They should be instructed to put a check mark under 100 for each series they recite correctly on the first try, under the 50 if they must hear it a second time to recite it correctly, and under the 0 if they must have it presented more than twice.